How to Ace Online, Video, or Zoom Interviews: Your Guide to Getting Hired

How to Ace Online, Video, or Zoom Interviews: Your Guide to Getting Hired

by
Peggy McKee

Contents

Letter from the Author 5

Introduction to Video Interviewing 7

Perfect the Tech 9

Set Up the Platform 9

Check Your Connections 12

Camera, Microphone, Speakers 14

Set the Scene 16

Lighting 18

Sound 19

Frame Yourself Well 20

Design Your Wardrobe 22

Over-Prepare for the Q&A 25

Research the Company 25

Rehearse Your Interview Answers 26

Job Interview Questions and Answers 29

Avoid Weak Language 42

Make a Cheat Sheet (or Two) 44

Create a 30-60-90 Day Plan 45

Have Questions to Ask 52

Do a Mock Interview 56

Interview Action! 58

Pump Up Your Energy.. 59

When to Sign On... 61

How to Start an Interview without a Traditional Handshake........ 61

Where to Look... 62

Practice Positive Body Language 63

Check Your Pace... 65

Ask for the Next Step 67

What If It's a Panel Interview?.. 69

Mistakes to Avoid—and How to Recover When You Can't........... 71

How to Follow Up 74

The Thank You Note 74

After the Note 76

Relax 78

Video Interview Checklist 80

BONUS – How to Answer 12 Unique Interview Questions About Remote Work.. 81

BONUS – Job Interview Prep Kit 90

Additional Resources.. 101

About the Author... 105

If You Liked This eBook, Please Give It 5 Stars! 106

Letter from the Author

Do you have an online interview set up? Chances are that you do, or that you will soon. Video interviewing is a skill everyone needs to develop. Employers are using online interviews to reduce costs, interview long-distance candidates, interview more people for the job, and social distance when there's a need.

There are wins here for you, too. A great online video chat shows that you're technologically adept, adaptable, confident, and have good communication skills. You can interview with more companies in less time to find the right job faster. And, because online work meetings are becoming an essential part of many jobs, all the skills you develop in video interviewing will help you communicate and perform well at work.

If you're having trouble getting your foot in the door of a company you'd like to speak with, you can even suggest a video call for a quick, convenient conversation. This can be a really impressive move, because most people won't think to do it. It's easier for them to say 'yes' to a quick video call than to say 'yes' to a full-on office meeting. It feels less formal and it takes less work to roll that into their schedule.

This book is for all levels of experience with video interviewing. If you've been out of the workforce for a while, we'll help you become more comfortable with this new challenge.

If you've used FaceTime, Facebook Messenger, Skype, or Zoom casually with friends and family, you'll gain insights into the unique qualities of using video for job interviewing, and avoid the small things that can make or break your video interview.

And if you've interviewed via video before, you'll still learn valuable tips and strategies to help you be even more effective. I'll walk you through all the steps to ace a video interview, stand out from other candidates, and get hired. You'll know how to manage the technical stuff, present your best self on camera, and avoid critical mistakes.

Plus, I've added 2 Bonuses for you: How to Answer Unique Questions for Remote Work (if you're interviewing for a work-from-home job), and a Job Interview Prep Kit!

Best of luck in your interview,

Peggy McKee, Executive Recruiter & Career Coach
CEO, Career Confidential
CareerConfidential.com

Introduction to Video Interviewing

Video interviews bring a new set of challenges to an already stressful event. The video piece may be new to you, or you may have had more Zoom meetings over the last year than you'd like. Either way, it's important to know everything you need to in order to put your best foot forward and get the job.

This book will help you do all that. First, we'll talk about how to set up the platform, why it's important to practice with it, and how to get all your technological ducks in a row. Then you'll learn how to show your best self on camera to the hiring manager in terms of lighting, sound and background. Hiring managers are paying close attention to how well you manage this piece.

After that, we'll dig into what you should wear, along with body language and speech patterns that especially stand out on video that could hurt you in this process. Because I know how important it is to over-prepare for any interview, I'll also give you some great tips for interview prep—from researching the company to composing and delivering interview answers that make you stand out.

I'll walk you through what to do in each step of the actual interview—from how to pump yourself up beforehand to understanding where to look to avoid the awkwardness so many job seekers have. And, I'll show you how to avoid and recover from several common problems and glitches.

Finally, I'll tell you how to follow up after this interview so you keep yourself moving forward in the hiring process.

Don't forget to find my Interview Prep Kit in the back, along with interview questions and answers specifically for remote work roles. I also want you to know that I offer interview and job search coaching:

Private, 1:1 Coaching
https://careerconfidential.com/peggy-mckee-career-coaching-special-offer/

Group Coaching Memberships
https://careerconfidential.com/coaching-memberships-nf/

Perfect the Tech

The first step to acing a video interview is to actually set it up so that you can be on video. Get all of the technology up and running and practice with it before the interview. This includes your video chat platform, computer connections, audio (speakers and microphone) and camera. The sooner you can do this, the better, because it's incredibly, remarkably, vitally important for you to practice an interview before the big day.

Set Up the Platform

When your potential new employer contacts you to set up the interview date and time, they'll tell you which video conferencing software they want to use. Typically, it will be Zoom or Skype, which you may have already, but there are several different video meeting apps available—including Facetime, Microsoft Teams, Google Meet, GoToWebinar, and Webex, among others.

Whatever it is, you need to familiarize yourself with it before your interview. Fumbling with it to make it work or accidentally turning on the filter that turns your face into a kitten's face will undermine you to an employer. You want to be calm, cool, collected, and in control.

For now, let's focus on Zoom and Skype, since they're the most commonly used. (Less common but also popular are Google Meet and Microsoft Teams—also easy to use.) It's possible to join a meeting just by clicking the link in an email invite, but it's better if you set up your own account so you can practice using it before your interview. You can even set up accounts for several platforms, just in case. It's easy and free, so you might as well take advantage of it.

Don't make the mistake of just using another person's account, because that can cause problems. I have, in fact, had someone try to interview with me by logging in with his significant other's account. Her name was quite different than his, and getting into the meeting with someone else's name was a little awkward. Not to mention, it made it seem as if he didn't care that much about this opportunity, because he didn't bother to take that one small extra step.

How do you set up an account? It's easy. Go to the website of the platform and follow the directions. For instance, if you'll be using Zoom, just go to Zoom's online site to sign up (Zoom.us). The website walks you right through everything you need.

My recommendation is to download the software onto the laptop or desktop you'll use for the interview. Even though you can use them through an app on your phone, it doesn't always work as well, and you lose some capabilities. In my opinion, those are worth using a laptop or desktop for. However, if you choose to use a phone, iPad or tablet, be sure to place it in a solid holder of some sort to keep it steady.

You'll use your email to sign up, so use the same professional, job-search-appropriate email that your prospective employer uses to contact you. You'll receive an email from Zoom with a link in it to click so you can activate your account. You'll set up your password, time zone (which is important so you don't accidentally miss a meeting set up in another time zone), and other details.

Then, you'll add your name and photo. The name you enter will be what shows up with your face in a Zoom meeting, before you turn on the video, or any time the video is off. Add the same photo you used for your LinkedIn profile, which should be a head and shoulders shot of you smiling in business appropriate attire.

Side Note: Most of the platforms are for straightforward video calls, which means you're speaking to someone in real time. Some employers use HireVue, which is a video interviewing company where you're not speaking to an actual person. You're simply given questions to respond to and you record your answers. The downside is that it can be unnerving to speak into what feels like a void with no feedback. The upside is that sometimes you get a couple of tries before your answer is recorded for good. Again, this is where practicing interview answers ahead of time, recording yourself on camera or working with a coach, will prove extremely helpful for you.

Set up what you'll be using as soon as possible and try out everything to see how it works. Then ask around in your network to see who can set up a short video call with you. Make those calls and get feedback on how you look and sound.

****

If you'd rather have a professional opinion or just keep your interview process confidential, I do personal interview coaching and can do a role play interview with you (and give you feedback on your interview answers) using Google Meet, Skype, or Zoom. I do one-on-one coaching (https://careerconfidential.com/peggy-mckee-career-coaching-special-offer/) and group coaching (https://careerconfidential.com/coaching-memberships-nf/).

****

Whoever you do your practice call with, it's incredibly important to get comfortable with the process and eliminate any technical glitches before you interview. The more you practice, the fewer mistakes you'll make and the more comfortable and confident you'll be.

Check Your Connections

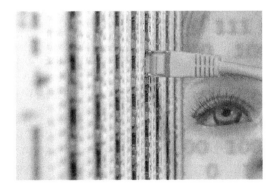

Recently, I coached a woman in Switzerland who wanted to practice interviewing for a major opportunity. When we got online, I noticed that as she moved her hands or her head, it left glowing trails of residual color across the screen. Not a professional look, and it would have cost her that high-level job for sure. However, it was a simple fix. Once she plugged her computer directly into her internet connection versus using wireless (WiFi), the trails were gone.

To avoid technical or psychedelic glitches in the first place, I recommend that your computer is also directly wired in (via ethernet cable) to the network, rather than using WIFI. If you're forced to use wireless, take the time to confirm you've got a strong signal. You may need to move physically closer to your router in order to get it. If you still have problems, an upgrade may be in order.

It's also a good idea to install any computer updates the day before the interview so your device is in peak form. The other day I got on a call with someone and their computer decided that was the moment to start an update, and it put us behind 15 minutes. That's OK with me as her interview coach, but that would not be OK with an interviewer.

You don't need a super powerful internet connection for video calls. I've seen recommendations for as little as 1.5 - 5 Mbps. Average connections are about 10 Mbps. The general rule is that if you can watch Netflix or YouTube on your computer with no buffering issues, you're fine for a video call. Practice calls will help you determine if you have enough power for a smooth conversation.

To ensure your system has plenty of bandwidth available during your interview, close all other applications and internet tabs that you don't need to have open during the interview. Ask others in your household to take a break from their own screen time while you're interviewing, too.

If you're using a laptop, check the battery power before the interview and if necessary, charge it before you start. Even better, keep it plugged in the entire interview so there's no chance to drain your battery. This is a big deal! I've done a lot of practice interviews with job seekers whose computer conked out on them in the middle of the call. That would be a disaster in an interview.

Finally, go ahead and get on your computer well in advance of your interview start time just to ensure everything is working properly and you don't run into any last-minute problems.

13

The idea you're going for here is to let no stone go unturned for any factor involved in your interview.

Camera, Microphone, Speakers

Camera quality is essential to how you look on screen to the interviewer. If your laptop has a good built-in camera, that's fine for you to use. Desktops won't have a built-in camera, so you'll have to buy one as an accessory and plug it in. To avoid all sorts of problems, always assume your camera is on.

Audio is a little different. Again, laptops will have a built-in microphone and speaker, and desktops won't. Your laptop may have a great microphone and speaker, or it may not. You might have to buy a separate microphone so you don't sound like you're talking in a cave. It all depends on your computer, and will show up when you do your practice calls. In my experience, a headset with a microphone gives the best sound quality regardless of whether you're using a laptop or desktop. That's important. The interview won't be wrecked if the video is a little fuzzy, but it will be a big problem if you and the interviewer can't hear each other. Logitech has some nice headsets, but other brands are good, too.

Also, right before you start, check to confirm that your camera, microphone and speakers work. I do Skype calls all the time, and it's amazing how often you can have technical issues that interrupt your conversation. But don't forget the basics, like simple cleaning. I did a practice interview with someone interviewing for a director-level opportunity and he looked fuzzy in the camera. What was it? A dusty lens! He didn't notice it, of course, but I sure did, and the CEO would have, too. Luckily, dusting your equipment is a simple fix.

To be safe, I would make a quick video call in the few minutes right before the interview to be sure everything's working properly. To be super-safe, you can even have a backup of all your equipment in case something conks out on you, so you can replace it without delaying the interview.

Set the Scene

**Please do all your interviews from home, or in as quiet and private a place as you can manage. You should absolutely never do any job interviews in a public place or on public WiFi. There are too many things that can go wrong with the connection, disruptions, and your privacy.

A good background is a significant piece of your call, because interviewers will notice what they see behind you and automatically make judgements about it.

In my opinion, the ideal background choice is a plain, solid-colored wall. The reason for that is that it keeps their focus on you, not on whatever's behind you. Even if you think it's beautiful, they may not, and it may distract them. And your decor isn't what matters in this situation, anyway—you and your fit for the job are all that matters. I once worked with an interior decorator who wanted to show off her room during her interview, even though she wasn't interviewing for a decorating job. I understood her inclination and even thought it was a nice room—but I did find it to be distracting.

If you don't have a plain wall available, then do the next best thing. Take action to guarantee that what they do see behind you is neat, clean, uncluttered, and attractive.

If your room is a mess, the implication is that you're a mess. They won't pay as much attention to what you're saying; they'll probably think that you don't pay attention to detail, you won't represent their company well, and therefore you can't be trusted with important business. That's what one college student found out when he interviewed with a truly massive bottle of whiskey on the table behind him. He didn't get the job.

Bookshelves are a common background choice, which is fine if they're arranged in an orderly way, and if you're far enough away so book titles aren't readable. Books are nice because they do show that you read—but they may spark a question about the latest book you read, so be prepared to talk about that, just in case.

It can also be acceptable to sit in front of a large piece of furniture (a plain wood cabinet would visually substitute for a wall) or a piece of neutral, non-controversial art. If you have no choice but to interview in your own living room or kitchen, that's OK but be sure it is scrupulously clean and uncluttered, even if you have to move a few items to another room.

If you're interviewing for remote work, it's a good idea to sit in your spotlessly clean and meticulously orderly home office (even if that's just a corner or a nook in your house). It shows them that you've already created a space that you can work in and be productive.

Some video platforms give you the chance to set a virtual background, but try not to use them. For interviews, a real background is best because it conveys a feeling of authenticity that a fake background doesn't.

Lighting

Lighting is a big, big deal. You need to be in a well-lit space with soft lighting coming toward your face that gives you good, balanced color and no shadows.

So, don't sit with your back to a window, because it puts your face in a shadow. And don't use the overhead lights, because that's not a great lighting angle. You could end up with an unattractive shine on your forehead, or worse, look like you're in an interrogation.

Ideal lighting would be soft natural light from a window in front of you, or slightly to the front/side. If you have blinds, adjust them so that you don't have lines of light and shadow across your face. Sheer curtains work really well for this because they diffuse light so well. But watch your angles here. Don't let half your face be shadowed. They need to see your whole beautiful, smiling face.

If you need artificial light, you have several good options. Many folks use a ring light (the circle lights that are set up behind your camera/screen). You can also try setting up two lamps on either side of your webcam so that the light on your face is even.

If you wear glasses, adjust the height of the lights so they don't bounce off in the wrong angle and cause a glare.

When you do your practice calls, be sure to ask how you look on screen in terms of your lighting.

Sound

Before any video interview, do a sound check. Aside from checking to confirm your speakers and microphone work, you must be absolutely sure there will be no background noise. You don't want to be interrupted by your spouse, your kids, your dog, or even any noise from outside. It's true that sometimes unavoidable things happen and you can recover from that, but the more you can do to dodge them in the first place, the better off you'll be in keeping your calm and focus on the interview.

Even if your dog is normally calm and quiet, don't take any chances. Put the dog outside or in the garage. Remove cats, birds, rabbits, and everything else that might bark, meow, chirp, flutter, or otherwise cause a distraction of any kind.

Close the windows and the doors. If you can't absolutely count on your family or roommates to stay out, strongly invite them to go somewhere else during your call. It might even be a great time for them to take the dog for a long walk.

Please turn off all notifications on your cell phone, just as you would in a face-to-face interview. It's best to turn it completely off, but at least make it silent, turn it face down and put it away from you.

No distractions!

Framing yourself well on camera is a big problem for many people. I recently coached an operations manager with an excellent resume and background, but who wasn't even getting past the first interview. He was so experienced and talented that I couldn't imagine why he'd have so much trouble—until I did a video interview with him and saw the issue. Not only did he never look into the eye of the camera, but he was also WAY too close to it. His face filled my screen like a floating head from a bad 1960s horror movie. I couldn't even see his neck, much less his shoulders. When we backed him up a bit, his interview outcomes changed immediately.

Ideally, this is how the interviewer will see you in his or her computer screen: a centered, head to chest portrait of their soon-to-be new hire. Leave a little space above your head so that your face is closer to the center of the screen.

This is a big thing to check on when you're doing your practice calls. Figure out where you need to be to get to that perfect framing. And watch where you're sitting in relation to what's behind you. Don't sit with your back too close to your wall or background. It looks awkward. Sit at least 3 feet away from whatever you're in front of. Again, if you're sitting in front of a bookshelf, sit far enough away so they can't read the titles because that can be distracting.

Also—the angle of your camera matters. I can't tell you how many people look down into the camera because the computer is on the desk in front of them. It's a natural thing to do, but try to avoid it. That upward viewing angle doesn't do anyone any beauty favors, and it sometimes forces the viewer to look up your nose. Not a good look.

Luckily, the fix is super easy: set your camera at eye level, or just a little bit higher, using whatever props you need to in order to make that happen. Stack up books or boxes to set your laptop on. Use a flexible tripod mount for your cell phone. Use any of those things to secure a webcam near your computer screen. Whatever you use, make sure it's very secure; the last thing you want is for your camera to fall during the interview.

Design Your Wardrobe

By now it's a cliché, but I actually know someone who tried to do a video interview wearing only a shirt, tie, and suit jacket...no pants. He thought, "they're only going to see me from the waist up, and this is more comfortable." Of course, he forgot he wasn't wearing pants and stood up in the interview to grab a piece of paper and they saw that he had no pants on. His chance at the job was over immediately.

For video interviews, you must dress just like you would for a regular interview—from head to toe.

The Suit

Especially for a first interview, your ideal interview attire should be conservative but stylish—not too trendy. Unless they specifically tell you to dress business casual, the gold standard for interviews is a matched suit made from wool or a wool blend. This means a jacket and pants, or jacket and skirt, although a jacket over a dress is also acceptable.

22

The ideal conservative color choices for men's suits are darker shades of gray and navy. Women have a little more latitude in color choices, but only in terms of the shade—so a lighter gray or blue could still look conservatively professional, but darker shades are almost always good, safe choices. The good news is that darker-colored suits are especially good for video interviews because video tends to wash out color.

Busy patterns are distracting on camera, so you'll want to wear a suit in either a solid color or a very subtle pattern. If you get a second or third interview and are able to dress more casually, it's still a good idea to stick with solid colors or subtle patterns (but no stripes).

The Shirt

What shirt goes best with your suit? For conservative fields like finance, accounting, healthcare, etc., wear a white or light blue shirt. For less formal or more creative fields like marketing, design, hospitality or education, you can wear a shirt in a brighter color or a pattern.

The Accessories

Ties should be a good quality silk in a solid color, stripe, or subtle pattern. No bowties, please.

Jewelry should also be simple for a conservative first interview. If you're using a headset, it may be uncomfortable to wear earrings, so it's OK to skip them. But if you do wear earrings, keep them simple and medium to small in scale. A necklace is fine, but don't wear any bracelets that will clink as you move your hands during the call. The microphone will amplify that sound.

Because the camera has a washout effect on color, you may want to rethink your makeup—maybe going a little darker or stronger to account for that issue—while still keeping a polished natural look on screen. Even if makeup is not something you normally wear, consider at least using a powder to reduce shine and a concealer if necessary. Cameras pick up a lot of flaws.

You may think you can skip wearing shoes because the interviewer will never see them, but I suggest that you put them on for the interview. They'll make you feel (and act) more like a business professional.

****

If you're not sure that you're presenting a professional image to potential employers, or if you'd like to practice your video interviews with professional feedback on your answers, I'd love to work with you as your coach to get you ready to ace any interview.

For **one-on-one coaching**, contact me at coachpeggymckee@gmail.com or send me a quick message on LinkedIn: https://www.linkedin.com/in/peggymckee1.
I always try to call people back as soon as possible, but if you have an interview coming up quick, let me know and I will make sure I get to you so you're ready.

If you'd like a **group coaching** experience (it often helps to see what's happening with other job seekers), I have regular online meetings which also helps you practice your video calls. Find out more here: https://careerconfidential.com/coaching-memberships-nf/

****

Over-Prepare for the Q&A

Preparation is vital for any successful job interview. The more prep work you do, the better off you'll be. You'll improve your answers, calm your nerves, and be perceived as more competent, informed, and intelligent. What's not to love about that?

What does good preparation look like? Research and rehearsal.

Research the Company

As soon as you have the interview scheduled, start researching the company. Use Google, LinkedIn, Twitter, Facebook, YouTube, the company website, and your own network to see what your friends or colleagues know about it.

What are you trying to find out? First, you're investigating the company. You're looking for what the company does, what their mission is, what their biggest challenges may be, what others think about it, and who their competitors are. How long have they been in business? How big are they and how are they structured? Do their employees like working for that company or is there a lot of turnover? Are there any press releases or news articles about them? What do they post on their social media pages?

But don't stop with only researching the company—also research the person who will be interviewing you. Look them up on LinkedIn. Where did they go to college? What's their work background? Where did they work before they got to this company? You may find things you have in common (a potential connection), or realize what part of your experience is best for you to emphasize in your call. This can make a really big difference.

Rehearse Your Interview Answers

Before any job interview, you'll do yourself a huge favor if you practice saying your answers *out loud* to common interview questions.

Rehearsing your answers helps you sound more natural and confident when you say them in the interview—especially if say, interviews make you nervous.

Why can't you put up scripts to read from since you're doing a video interview? Because you need to look into the camera when you speak (more on that later) and because you don't want to seem like you're reading something out loud. Most people don't read out loud with a natural-sounding rhythm and tone. When they realize you're reading answers instead of speaking to them, you could also give the impression that you didn't bother to prepare or that you aren't taking this seriously.

You can, however, jot down some words or phrases that jog your brain to remember important points to mention. These are easy to tape to your computer screen edge or have on your desk to glance at before you answer. These kinds of cheat sheets are great for phone interviews as well as video interviews.

What kinds of things should you mention? The key to delivering job-winning interview answers is to think about yourself as a product that will help them do a job. Your task is to tell them about the product and show them how purchasing this product (hiring you for that role) will benefit them and the company. That's the idea behind 'selling yourself for the job.'

All the research you do on the company, the job, and the interviewer helps you gather that information on what it is that they need and are looking for. You'll add to that knowledge by asking questions in the interview. With everything you learn, you can target what you say to them to be so incredibly effective in your interview that they offer you the job.

One great way to communicate your value is through stories about events or experiences in your career that highlight skills or strengths that make you someone they'd want to hire. Employers want to hear about your triumphs, and about how you developed strength through overcoming adversity, so they ask behavioral interview questions that start with, "Tell me about a time when…" Have some of those stories handy, too.

The best way to tell stories in job interviews is by using the STAR method. STAR stands for:

S – Situation
T – Task
A – Action
R – Result

Here's how to use it in your interview: Describe the **S**ituation you were in or the **T**ask you were presented with in order to provide context. Then talk about the **A**ction you took to address it, and the thought process you went through to reach that decision. Finally, describe the **R**esults you achieved. The results are the most important piece, so don't forget to include them.

Structurally, an answer in this format would sound (in an extremely general way) something like, "Once, my team faced X situation and we needed a solution fast because of Y. I came up with the idea to take X action, and as a result, we saved the company X dollars/saved the customer relationship and they rewarded us with X business."

Side note: your interview answers should always be delivered in a positive way that never, ever disparages your former co-workers, bosses, or companies.

Job Interview Questions and Answers

Here are some examples of good interview answers.

Tell me about yourself.

This is the most typical job interview starter question. Some job seekers misunderstand it as an icebreaker, which causes them to answer it as if they were in a social setting: 'I'm married with 2 kids, I like rock climbing, I'm the world's most devoted Red Sox fan,' or whatever. That's not the right answer.

This is one of the questions I spend the most time on as a coach with my job seeker clients. Why? Because this is the foundation that your entire interview rests on. Get it wrong, and you'll spend the whole interview catching up or correcting assumptions they made from your answer. Get it right, and you've laid a very smooth, solid foundation to build on.

It's important for you to use this opportunity to deliver a unique selling statement—a quick summary of why they should hire you for this job. In the rest of the interview, you'll go into that in a more in-depth way with answers to other questions.

To structure this answer, think about the job and the company, and put yourself in the hiring manager's shoes. What would you want to hear from someone you were trying to hire for this role? Think about this in terms of your background, accomplishments, and maybe even a personality trait or two that speak to why you're a good fit.

So, you could talk about your education, where you've worked and what you did while you were there. Highlight promotions, awards, important skills, or significant accomplishments—especially those that would be directly beneficial for this job.

What does that sound like in an answer? Here are 3 examples:

(1)
"I was born and raised in Texas, and attended the University of Oklahoma where I received my Bachelor's Degree in Accounting. My first position was at ABC Company, where I did X, Y, and Z. I was recruited into EFG Company, where I did X and was promoted for Y. Last year, I was recognized with a company award for my contribution to X."

(2)
"I'm from California, but I went to school at the University of Arizona and got my Bachelor's degree in Biochemistry and then an MBA. My first two jobs were in X field, but then I became interested in Y, so I enrolled myself in some training classes and switched over. I've been successful in this new arena, and have accomplished ABC. One of the things that caught my attention about this job was X, because I know I could really use my skills in ABC here to grow X for you."

(3)
"After graduating early from college and immediately entering my last firm, through hard work and consistently selling among the top reps in my territory, I was able to make manager in one year. I think that my performance results and experience with XYZ product and ABC customers, would make me a great fit for this company. I feel that I could immediately have a significant positive impact here."

Tell your story, and bring up the information that will matter most to them. Keep your answer within a minute or two, so if you have a long work history, you'll have to edit. The goal is to essentially say, 'I'm skilled, I'm accomplished, and I can do great things for you in this role.'

Why did you leave your last job?

This can be a little bit of a minefield, because most people don't leave a job that's still a positive situation for them. But speaking in a negative way about your former employer is a big no-no, because it reflects badly on you, not them.

If you're leaving a job that you're still employed in, you have a few good options. One is to simply say something like, "I've enjoyed my time there, but I'm ready to use my skills in a more challenging role and this one seems like a great fit." A similar way to say that is: "I've loved working at Acme, but this opportunity is what I've always wanted to do because of X, and I just can't pass up the chance."

If the roles are too similar for you to say that convincingly, you could name a non-blaming, neutral factor in your old job you'd like to get away from that isn't part of this new job. For instance, you could pick on traveling: "My old job required a lot of travel, which was great for a while, but I'm ready to be home more."

If you lost your job through no fault of your own, like through a mass layoff or restructuring, just say that. "The company laid off a large section of workers and I got caught in it." Then you can allay any fears they might have about you by saying, "My old boss would be happy to speak with you about my performance there."

****

If you've been fired, or are leaving a difficult situation, working with a coach on how to word that can help you tremendously.

I worked with one gentleman who was so upset by getting fired that he stuttered when he talked about it and didn't even realize it. So

31

that meant that he wasn't getting offers, which battered his confidence. We worked together to talk about that and come up with an explanation he felt good about, and he got a job offer almost immediately after that.

Contact me at coachpeggymckee@gmail.com or find me on LinkedIn: https://www.linkedin.com/in/peggymckee1.

****

Why do you want to join this company?
Why do you want to work here?

Employers want to know your motivation for working with them, and this is a great chance to show your enthusiasm for this job.

Definitely focus on the positive aspects of this organization. Don't make the mistake of bringing up negative aspects of your old company that you want to get away from by taking this job: "This company offers X and my old one hasn't made it to this century. I can't wait to get out of that mess and into this company that understands what's needed." I've heard job seekers say things like that in an effort to establish rapport but it's misguided and will reflect badly on you.

This is your chance to simply tell them what appeals to you about this company and this job and more importantly, why you and your skills are a good fit for it. So, your answer should focus on why you're enthusiastic about this opportunity and using your skills in X, Y, and Z in this role.

For example, you might say:

"Based on my research, I'm impressed with what you've done in X and even more interested in your plans for Y. I feel that this company is one where my background in A, B, and C will be put to good use. My strengths in A, B, and C will absolutely help me help you reach your goals."

If you'll notice, this answer focuses on why you're happy to help them—rather than on why this job helps you. If this job has a personal appeal to you, it's fine to briefly mention that in your answer, but keep the main focus on what you can do for them. Tell them the benefits of hiring you.

What's your greatest weakness?

Hiring managers always ask about your weaknesses in one form or another. It's an annoying but fair question. No one is without a weakness, and it reveals a lot about you in what you say and how you say it.

The weaknesses question leaves a lot of room for error. Some candidates point out a fake weakness, like, "I work too many hours," or "I'm such a perfectionist," and that doesn't do them any favors. Others actively hurt themselves by talking about real weaknesses that will hold them back in this job—like saying they're not good with details while interviewing for a project management job.

Your overall goal in confessing to a weakness is to name some trait or quality that isn't necessary for your success in this role.

My favorite option is to talk about a real weakness that may affect your personal life that works in your favor in this particular job. For instance, when I interviewed for sales roles, I always used impatience as my answer. No one can say that impatience isn't a problem. In fact, it's caused me several problems in my personal relationships. However, my impatience always caused me to be more aggressive and push for the sale, and I was really successful at it.

What are your strengths?

This question is a great opportunity to highlight why they should want to hire you. To answer it, think about the things this hiring manager is looking for in terms of skill sets, relationships, background, character traits, and so on. Think about what it takes be successful in this role, and point out those things that you have in your answer.

Maybe this job takes an incredible amount of work—so naturally, you'd point out your work ethic, possibly with a story of when you went above and beyond to accomplish a goal the company needed. Maybe it's requires tremendous communication skills—give an example of a time you communicated well and saved or corrected a difficult situation. Maybe there's a quick learning curve—so go through how you'll get up to speed quickly, like with a 30-60-90-day plan (more on that later). Maybe there's a new thing the company wants to set up, so you'll talk about when you've done something similar before, or you have the transferable skills to help them do it.

Know how your skill set equals the skill set required for this position, and then deliver a concise but detailed statement that explains that. Show them that you fit, plus even a little bit more. Provide a few examples of what you've done in the past that you can do again for them. What have you achieved or accomplished that make you a great fit for this role?

Always tie your answer to your fit for the job.

Tell me about a time when you failed.

The bad news is that you can't say you've never failed. But it's OK. Everybody fails at one time or another. If you've never failed, it means you've never taken a risk (or made much progress, either) or you've never made a mistake (which is impossible). What's important is that you learn from it and don't make the same mistake twice.

The ideal story to tell is about a real failure that you learned from and transform into a comeback story with an ending that shows how you've improved in your role because of it.

Here's an example: "Once I missed a project deadline because it just got lost in the shuffle. I never wanted that to happen again, so I took a course to learn my Outlook program in greater detail so that I could stay better organized and always be on time. It was a good move because I've actually been much more productive since then and more effective for my organization."

Here's another: "I'm naturally optimistic, which is great for my attitude and ability to work with people, but once it caused me to overlook a potential problem with my project that turned into an actual problem. Since then, I always come up with a contingency plan no matter how optimistic I feel about it. And actually, it's been great because I have even more peace of mind because I know that I've always got a Plan B, just in case."

Answers like these show that you're not afraid to admit a mistake, and you're always interested in improving yourself and your performance. Those are attractive qualities to an employer.

How do you rate yourself as a professional?

If they ask you how you rate yourself on a scale of 1 to 10, should you say you're an 11? Some people would say yes, but the truth is that you probably shouldn't. It could make you seem arrogant or insincere. What sounds reasonable, sincere and positive? Probably a 6, 7, or 8, depending on where you are in your career. Why? Because it makes you seem as if you understand that you have room to grow and develop—and don't we all?

If you're a recent graduate interviewing for an entry-level job, you should answer 6 or 7. That's better than average, with room to learn.

If you're further along in your career, answer 7 or 8. Only a true Subject Matter Expert with extensive experience should rate themselves a 9 or a 10.

But here's the important part: once you answer, give them your explanation. Say, "On a scale of 1 to 10, I see 5 as a true average, and a 10 as perfect. I believe I'm better than average, and no one's perfect."

Then you can expand on it a little by talking about how you rate yourself compared to others in the same roles, or what things you've accomplished. If you can give a sincere, reasoned response, you'll stand out from other candidates and earn big points with the interviewer.

How does this position fit with the career path you see for yourself?

This is a difficult question to answer, and a lot of candidates shoot themselves in the foot with it. You may not know what career path you want just yet, and that's OK, but you don't want to just blurt that out. It could make it seem like you're floating with no plan or drive, and it doesn't leave a great impression. Employers want people who are motivated, and who have a reason for wanting this particular job.

So, a good answer would focus on what this job will teach you and how it will help you reach general career goals, such as:

"I would say that this position is a growth role that will benefit me professionally because I'll be learning and developing valuable skills. I want to grow and be able to contribute more and be more than I am today. As I hone my skills and do well, I'll benefit both financially and personally, in terms of job satisfaction. I'll move into roles of greater responsibility, and that's what I want."

If you have a more specific destination in mind, that's great, and you can talk about how this job is going to help you meet that goal.

A warning: don't say that you'd eventually like to end up in their job, because in some instances that could pose a threat to them. If the company is a small one, there may be no where for them to go. Or they may not want to move up because they're camped out happily where they are.

You don't have to know your exact path now. Many opportunities come up that we can't plan for, and we learn more about what we want along the way. But you do want to try to show why you want this job.

Why should we hire you?

This can be tough to answer if you're modest or even a little unsure of yourself in going after this job. However, you need to remember that the job interview is a sales process. Imagine yourself as a product that will take care of whatever task or problem this employer has, and tell the hiring manager why you'd be good to have on site to solve it.

To do this, you need to understand and be able to articulate what you offer. Know how your skill set equals the skill set required for this job, plus at least one good thing you bring that makes you unique or desirable over other candidates. Why a plus one thing? It's to show that you will not only meet their expectations, you'll exceed them. This gives you an edge over your competition.

Talk about one or two of your accomplishments that highlight how you're a great candidate (based on the job skills required). Talk about how they'll see that you're a good fit for the company when they speak with your references (they're like a review). Please prep your references before the interview so they have a heads up for what to say that would be helpful and you know what they're going to say about you.

For example, you might say something like, "You should hire me because I have the skills plus some, I've done the work before successfully, I'm going to fit in well with this company and perform successfully in this role, and that's what you want; do you agree?"

Note: asking "Do you agree?" helps you understand if you gave them the information they needed (and give them more information if you need to) and helps to nudge them along to making you the offer.

What is good customer service?

This is a natural question for direct customer service roles in retail, hospitality, or call center roles, but a wide range of other positions also have significant customer contact in accounting and finance, sales, technology, healthcare, education, and so on. Really, any business with customers wants to offer good customer service.

So first, recognize how important you are to their customer's experience and to the company's reputation. If you work for that company, then you're the face of the company. Your interaction with them will affect how they feel about the company, whether or not they come back, and whether or not they recommend it to others.

To elevate this answer into a job winner, show this employer that you understand this dynamic and talk about customer delight.

What does that mean? It means going beyond an OK but not great answer like, "Good customer service is friendly and helpful," or "being knowledgeable about my product or service and able to help customers make good decisions."

In my opinion as a former sales rep and current career coach, the best answer would sound more like: "Good customer service delights the customer. It's less about what you or I say is good, or what the company says it's good. It's what the customer says is good. The most important thing is to make the customer so happy that they refer you to someone else. To know that I reached that, I always ask if I provided what they were looking for from this call or visit. So that I can make sure I'm providing what they need so they will be delighted with us."

If you were a tree, what kind of a tree would you be?

Why do employers ask weird questions like these? Mostly, it's because they want to see how you'll react to something out of left field. Sometimes, it's because they want an insight into your personality.

Remember that every interview answer is a chance to keep selling yourself for the job, and this one is no exception. So, don't blow off this question by just talking about a tree you like. Talk about a tree that could illustrate qualities that would be good for someone to have in this job.

For instance, a fruit tree may be a good choice because you could say that it's productive. Oak trees are considered strong and dependable. You could say that evergreen trees are steady because they're always the same, no matter the season. Or, that palm trees are flexible in the stresses of the wind and able to withstand strong storms.

Try to stay away from trees that could be interpreted to have negative qualities. A weeping willow can seem graceful to some but

38

alternatively, can easily seem sad. Cottonwood trees are flexible, but also produce a lot of debris that others have to clean up.

If you go blank, you could try for some humor and say something like, "I want to be the tree that would be the most useful and productive for this organization. That's my goal."

If they ask you what animal you'd be, go through the same thought process. Choose something with qualities you want to highlight in yourself to show that you're a good fit for this job.

A fun way to end your answer is to ask, "What did you choose when they asked you this question in your interview?"

What are your workplace values?

With this answer, show what kind of person you are, why they should trust you, why you'll be a great hire, what you'll be like to work with, or anything else that will help to sell you for the job.

Focus on what your values are in relation to work, not your personal life, unless these specifically align. Here are some good answers:

- "I do what I say I'm going to do, I follow up on my commitments, and I think of others before I think of myself."
- "I always do the best I can, because my employer is paying for a service, and I supply that just like I would if I owned a business and that person was my customer. My customer deserves the best I can deliver."
- "I believe that everyone who works for a company is part of a team, and it's important that we support each other and do what we need to so we can get the job done. I try to lead by example in that way."

Your pre-interview research will pay off here. What are their corporate values? Talk about which of your values align with theirs.

Please be honest, because something that isn't truthful won't serve you in the end. If your values don't line up with theirs, you won't be happy working there. Their core values will have a major effect on your career. Avoid organizations with toxic values or an environment that will make you miserable.

What do you expect from a supervisor?

Why should you watch out when answering this? You don't know what this supervisor's management style is, so you don't want to step on their toes. You need to be careful to say nothing negative about any previous boss, even in a backhanded way. For instance, don't say things like, "I expect a boss who doesn't yell at people," or "I expect a supervisor who doesn't play favorites." It will make you look worse than any view they may have about your last boss.

Be positive and generic. Think of it as a short wish list and name 2-3 qualities that any good supervisor might have: good communication skills, a sense of humor, knowledge, leadership skills, loyalty, fairness, etc.

For example, I might say, "I expect a supervisor to communicate clearly, treat me fairly, and give me opportunities to do as much as I can for the organization." This answer also shows my desire to contribute and achieve within that company.

Other good answers might sound like:

"I would expect a supervisor to keep the lines of communication open with me and offer feedback when I'm doing a good job and when I have room for improvement."

"I would hope that a supervisor could have a sense of humor, be adaptable to employee work styles, and be willing to help employees develop additional skills to be more successful."

What salary are you looking for?

Before we talk about how to answer this question, please understand that you should never, ever, ever bring up any question or comment about money until they offer you the job.

However, it's very common for employers to ask you about salary before they invest too much time interviewing you. You have a few options for how to answer it—by trying not to answer it.

You can deflect with humor, which I've done myself. Smile and say, "Does that mean you're offering me the job?"

Or, you can deflect in a more straightforward way: "I'm really interested in learning more about the job and telling you more about me so that we can see if this role is a good fit before we start talking about money."

As a third option, you can simply say, "I'm really interested in this job, and I'm sure you will offer a salary that's commensurate with the responsibilities of the role."

If they push back and insist on a number, try asking them what their budget is for the job, or what their expected range is. Because they do have a budget they have set aside for that salary. If their number range is acceptable to you, you can say, "I'm sure we can come to an agreement on money if we decide that I'm the right person for this job."

Your goal is to get them to want to hire you first—and then you talk about the money. If they don't want to hire you, the money doesn't matter anyway.

One of the hallmarks of a video interview, like phone interviews, is that some of the things that may blend in a little when you're sitting across from them in person can stand out in stark relief when you're on the phone or on screen. Weak language is one of those things.

What's weak language? It's made up of common, throwaway words and phrases that many people use without thinking twice about it. They're terrible to use in job interviews.

- I Hope
- Hopefully
- With luck
- Possibly
- If possible
- I will try
- If all things go well

Even though these phrases seem natural and fine, they're actually interview killers. You just can't say in a job interview, "I hope I can" or "I'll try my best to handle the job."

The employer doesn't care if you hope or if you'll try—they want to know that you can and you will. Anything else makes them feel like they'd be taking a risk by hiring you.

Train yourself to use strong phrases and power words like:

- *I will*
- *I have*
- *I can*
- *I know*

Remember Yoda: "There is no try—only do or do not."

Similarly, don't undermine your credibility with hesitations and filler words such as:

- Like
- you know?
- um…
- sort of…
- I guess?

Train yourself to speak with confidence, and to be comfortable with the silence. You always want convey confidence in your ability to accomplish the tasks of this role.

****

If you'd like to practice your interview answers, or need help with specific answers for your field or the jobs you're interviewing for, I'd love to work with you as your interview coach. Find out more about individual coaching (https://careerconfidential.com/peggy-mckee-career-coaching-special-offer/) or a group coaching membership (https://careerconfidential.com/coaching-memberships-nf/).

****

Make a Cheat Sheet (or Two)

Just like in a phone interview, a video interview is an ideal chance to sneak a few notes in to keep you on track. Your notes could include a few important phrases you want to remember to say, important numbers that illustrate your accomplishments, or a copy of your resume.

Remember, the interviewer won't be able to see anything the camera can't see. So, you're free to keep your cheat sheets on your desk, propped (securely) up near the screen so you can see them, or even as post-it notes stuck directly on your computer screen.

Create a 30-60-90 Day Plan

When I met Wayne, he was a project leader who'd been laid off because of the pandemic. He was discouraged, because he'd expected and wanted to advance in his career at that company. His goal was to be a manager or director with more responsibility and more pay, but he was concerned that he'd have to go into a new job at the same level as before and work his way back up.

The reason I met him is because he hired me to coach him through this transition. We started by upgrading his resume and LinkedIn profile, along with his cover letter and messaging to hiring managers so he could get interviews. We practiced those interviews on video, both so he could practice with this method and so we could record them. By recording them, he was able to go over them again several times before our next coaching session. Ultimately, he did land the job he wanted at the director level with a $27,000 pay raise from his last job.

****

If you'd like to schedule coaching with me for a similar experience, please email me at coachpeggymckee@gmail.com or find me on LinkedIn: https://www.linkedin.com/in/peggymckee1

****

All the things we did with his resume, LinkedIn profile, and interview practice helped him tremendously, but the crowning touch to all of those things was that we developed a 30-60-90-day plan that he could present and go over in the interview.

The executive team he interviewed with said specifically that his plan helped them be very comfortable in extending the offer for that job, even though it was at a higher level than what he'd done before.

What is a 30-60-90 Day Plan?

Basically, a 30-60-90-day plan is a detailed outline of the actions you plan to take in the first 3 months of your new job. You show this plan in the interview and talk it over with the hiring manager so that you make sure you know what they want and they can see you clearly being successful in the job.

When you do the research required to make a detailed plan like this, all your interview answers become stronger because you're more informed. You know what their problems are and how you could help solve them.

A 30-60-90-Day Plan is by far the most powerful item you can bring to any interview to help them see you as smart, capable, and credible. It builds their trust in you. These plans are so unbelievably effective that I personally would never let my job seekers go to an interview without one.

Remember that for the company, hiring is a risk. They can make an educated guess as to what kind of employee you'd be, but they can't really know until you get there. By doing the work to create a plan before you even have an offer, you demonstrate that you're not afraid to work hard. You're doing something that isn't required before they even hire you, because it will help you be successful for them. They'll see that they can look forward to having someone who's take-charge, thoughtful, focused, and dedicated to success.

A plan also demonstrates a host of soft skills that employers want. You'll highlight your critical thinking and organizational skills because you're prioritizing tasks and setting goals. You'll also show your communication skills just through the back-and-forth conversation involved in walking them through your plan. It will be a deeper, more involved discussion than they're having with other candidates.

It helps you build rapport and show interest, too. The fact that you took the time to make a plan will get their attention and they'll see that you care a lot about getting this role and being successful in it.

And if you don't have much experience, a plan helps you get over that hump. You'll show the knowledge you do have about it and that you're capable of doing the job. Many, many job candidates have beat out others with more experience by using a plan.

Why is it so effective in all these different ways? It's because it lets the hiring manager, in effect, take you for a test drive. Think about the last time you went car shopping. If you think about it, they try not to spend too much time talking to you about the car before they offer you a test drive. Why is that? It's because if you drive the car, you're more likely to buy it. Walking them through your 30-60-90-day plan is like giving them a test drive. If they 'try you out' by talking through what you'd do on the job, they can visualize it. They get comfortable with it. They are much more likely to offer you the job.

What's in 30-60-90-Day Plan?

Every job has things that need to be done in order for you to be successful in it. List these 90-day action items out as specifically as possible, with about one page per 30-day section.

First 30 Days
The first 30 days usually focus on getting your bearings, getting to know people, and training–learning the company systems, procedures, people, products, services, software, vendors, and/or customers.

So, most of the items in the 30-day section should be along the lines of attending training sessions, mastering product or service knowledge, learning specific corporate systems or software, traveling to learn your territory (if you're in sales), meeting other members of the team, reviewing accounts, etc.--all the things you'd need to do to get started strong. Not every boss has a lot of time to train you, so if you can show how you can get up to speed on your own, they love it. They'll see that they don't have to hold your hand; you can take charge of doing what you need to do.

Second 30 Days (the 60 Day part)

The next 30 days often focus on simply digging deeper—more field or independent time, more involvement in issues, more customer or vendor introductions, reviews of customer satisfaction, reviews of procedures, and so on. More details, more responsibility. A big point here in this 60-day section is getting feedback from your manager to see how you're doing. Put this in your plan.

The Last 30 Days (the 90 Day part)

The last 30 days are the "taking off on your own" part. By now, you should be up to speed, independent, and significantly contributing to the organization. You should be initiating things on your own, like increasing customers or revenue, generating ideas to save time or money, implementing plans or schedules (based on your reviews and input from before), fine-tuning your schedule, and continuing to get performance feedback.

This 90-day section really highlights what you're bringing to the game. What can you do for them? By the time you get to this point, your hiring manager will be picturing you in the job...and already thinking about hiring you.

Some jobs will want you to move faster or slower than this, depending on their circumstances. That's OK. This is a framework to lay out your ideas and can be adjusted as needed.

Include details

The more details you can incorporate into your plan, the better. That means, investigate to try and find out things like the name of the software they use, and put that into your 30-day section. Find the name of the training they put new employees through, and include that.

How do you find this kind of information? Read over the job description and the company website. Google searches are good, but LinkedIn, Twitter and Facebook can be gold mines. Look at the company's corporate pages and posts, as well as those of employees or groups.

Worried about getting it wrong?

You may be afraid to create a plan because you don't want to make a mistake in the interview. Don't be afraid. The hiring manager could never expect a plan like this to be perfect, because you haven't worked there.

Perfect isn't the point. The point is to use it as a high-level conversational piece in your interview. The discussion is what matters and what helps them see you in the job. They'll be impressed by what you got right, and give you feedback on what you missed the mark on. That conversation alone will elevate you above your competition for this job.

How can you use a 30-60-90-Day Plan in a video interview?

In a typical, in-person job interview, you'd sit next to the hiring manager, going over a paper copy of your plan and making notes. So how do you translate that to a video interview?

You may be able to share your screen in order to show them your plan. You'd simply say, "I've put a lot of thought into how I would approach this job in the first 90 days, and I put together an action plan that I'd like to share with you. Can I go over it with you?" Practice the screen sharing feature in your pre-interview calls so you get the steps down for how to manage that smoothly. This feature is available in GoToMeeting, Zoom, Skype, Google Hangouts, and others.

In fact, I recently worked with a woman who interviewed for a high-level Sales Director job over several countries, and she built out a 90-day, 180-day, 365-day plan (because it was a very big job). She presented it in Zoom and was very comfortable with moving between screens and talking about her ideas. As she was presenting it, she asked if she was on target and if they could see her plan as an effective strategy. They were impressed with her plan and asked her for a copy, which she emailed to them. All of this made them extremely comfortable with the prospect of working with her and giving her responsibility for a high-level role.

What happens if you can't screen-share your plan or if they don't want to see it in your first interview? You can still use the enormous knowledge you gain from creating it to give more effective answers about how you would approach this job. Those beefed-up, targeted answers will help you move forward.

If you're not sure you'll be receiving a second interview much less an offer (and you want one), you might consider attaching your plan to your thank you note, once you amend it with what you learned in the interview. That may be what makes you stand out from your competition!

****

Read more about 30-60-90-day plans on my website:
https://careerconfidential.com/how-to-create-the-best-30-60-90-day-plan-for-your-job-interview/
Or get my proven 30-60-90-Day Plan Template with detailed strategies for writing and using it in any job interview. Each plan comes with an optional personal review of your completed plan and a 100% money-back guarantee.

Action Plan (for any white-collar job)
https://careerconfidential.com/306090-action-plan-product-reviews/

Sales Plan (for sales roles)
https://careerconfidential.com/306090-sales-plan-product-reviews/

Manager Plan (for management-level and above)
https://careerconfidential.com/30-60-90-day-plan-for-managers-product-reviews/

Executive Plan (for Directors, VPs, CEOs, etc.)
https://careerconfidential.com/30-60-90-day-plan-for-executives-product-reviews/

****

Have Questions to Ask

Asking questions is an important part of any job interview. You'll need to ask questions to clarify information, keep the conversation going, and gather information for yourself to determine if this is the right job for you.

Video interviews can bring unique communication challenges. Lag times can cause you to speak over each other, and sometimes you may miss a word or two in their question or comment. The easiest way to deal with these issues is to get comfortable asking questions that clarify for understanding.

You may want to clarify that you understood what they said, by repeating the question as you heard it. You may need more information than they just gave you in their answer. You may even just have a comment that expands on or agrees with what they just said. Those kinds of questions or responses are a normal part of conversations, and they should be part of interviews, too. Good communication skills establish rapport and help them see you as someone they could work with.

Beyond the basics, you do want to make sure you have specific questions to ask them in the interview. Not only will you seem more engaged and intelligent, you'll get valuable information to help you move forward or decide whether to take the job.

Depending on whether this is a first or second interview, there are a variety of good questions to ask. Some are better to ask in the beginning, and some at the end.

2 great questions to ask near the beginning of your interview:

If the absolute ideal, perfect person for the job walked in right now, what skills or experience would they have?

On the surface, that may seem like a scary thing to ask because you're afraid you'll come up short in the comparison to the ideal. But really, everyone would come up short. It's their ideal.

So why do should you ask it? Because their answer gives you a blueprint for stronger answers to their questions. By tailoring your answers as closely as possible to what they say, they'll be more targeted and more effective.

So, for example, if they say they want X, Y, and Z skills. You may have X and Y, which you can easily point out, but you don't have Z exactly the way they verbalized to you. But you do have a similar skill that could transfer to fill that need. They may not see it unless you point it out. And you may not know to point that out without the blueprint.

The job description alone doesn't always address this issue. Sometimes the job description is a little out of date. Sometimes the hiring manager has a few things more important to them personally than others, and so that's what they'll mention when they answer this question. Having an insight like this into the mind of the hiring manager is an incredibly valuable interview success tool.

Why is the position open? / What happened to the last person in this role?

Find out whether the last person left, or was promoted or fired. If they were promoted, it's a great idea to ask what it was that they did that made them so successful in the company. That will give you real clues as to how you can be successful, as well.

Mid-interview, you may want to ask questions like these:

What are the most immediate challenges I would be facing in this position?
The challenges they mention can tell you so much. Maybe they want the impossible, which could be your signal to run far and fast away from this position. More likely, they'll give you a golden opportunity to talk more specifically about why you're the perfect person to meet those challenges.

Their answer could also be a great lead-in for you to begin discussing your 30-60-90-day plan to show how you'd begin to accomplish those goals.

How do you measure performance or evaluate success in this role?
What accomplishments do they care about most? How do they conduct performance reviews? It's helpful to know the rules of the game before you play. Find out what's most important to them and what to expect.

What do you like best about this company?
This is such a great question. You could learn about popular benefits or perks, or a company culture you'll love (or not). If they have trouble coming up with something quickly, consider that a red flag.

Here's the best question to ask at the end of your interview, phrased two different ways:

Do you have any concerns about me for this role?
Do you see me as someone who could be successful in this role?
This is called a closing question. Remember that the job search is like a sales process? This is the question that asks for the sale. Are they

ready to make the decision to go with you? It can feel like a hard question to ask, but it's incredibly valuable.

If they think you could be successful there, you know you've done well and gotten at least a mental commitment to offering you the job. If they have concerns, right now is your best chance to address them and potentially save your job offer. Once you exit the interview, that becomes exponentially more difficult, if not impossible.

What questions never to ask

Never, ever, ever, ever ask about money, benefits, or time off during the interview. Period. Those are all negotiation points for after you get the offer.

Do a Mock Interview

Before your first video interview, do a few practice calls. Check your background, lighting, and sound to make sure they're good to go. Check yourself to make sure you look good on screen and that you're not fidgeting and have good body language. Most importantly, get used to looking into a camera lens while you speak instead of into the interviewer's face. If you're not very comfortable with it, it can make you nervous, so practice, practice, practice video calls before your interview.

Whether you've interviewed on video before or not, you'll do yourself a favor if you do a practice run before the big day. Record yourself so you can go back on a post-call analysis to see what you need to improve. The more you answer interview questions and know what you're going to say, the more confident you'll be. Once you can see and hear what your answers sound like, you'll be able to refine them and make them more powerful.

Mock interviewing works. Here are examples from my experience that prove it: A plant manager from Wisconsin who was getting interviews but no offers spent 3 hours in coaching sessions with me (and practiced on his own through replaying our recorded sessions). In his very next interview, he got the job with a significant pay bump over what he had before. A sales rep practiced with me and landed a higher paying job with bigger bonuses than what she had ever received, as well.

This kind of story happens all the time. The practice helps, but I'm also a firm believer in getting an expert to help you. If the check engine light comes on in your car, you get it fixed faster and better by going to a mechanic for help than by watching YouTube videos to figure out how to fix it yourself.

****

If you'd like to run through a mock interview with a career coach and get professional feedback for an important job interview, schedule some coaching time with me:
https://careerconfidential.com/peggy-mckee-career-coaching-special-offer/

If you'd rather speak with me about it first, please email me at coachpeggymckee@gmail.com or find me on LinkedIn:
https://www.linkedin.com/in/peggymckee1
****

Interview Action!

Before you start, close every other tab on your computer. Take no chances with interruptions to your connection as well as popups, notification dings, or anything else that could distract you. Make sure your home screen looks good—just in case the video fails and they get a look at it.

If you have a large monitor, you could consider having your resume or cheat sheet notes on screen next to the video—just for quick reference. Or, just print them out and put them on the table next to you, out of range of the camera. Have some water (no ice, no clinking) near you in case your throat gets dry from talking.

Just like the camera drains some color, it can drain some of the energy and enthusiasm they perceive from you. So, turn up your energy level just a little bit for this call.

Before the interview starts, do a few jumping jacks, a quick walk, or practice some power poses. The most well-known advocate of power poses is Dr. Amy Cuddy, a Professor at Harvard Business School. In 2012, she delivered what came to be a wildly popular TED talk, called "Your Body Language Shapes Who You Are," where she shares her research on power poses.

What's a power pose? Think Wonder Woman, feet apart with your hands on your hips. Another is a victory pose, which is holding your arms up in the air in a "V" with your chin slightly raised like you just won a race.

Basically, her team found that spending 2 minutes in a power pose can decrease cortisol (the stress hormone) and increase testosterone (which boosts risk-taking, which is a function of confidence).

People who tried it before job interviews performed better than those who didn't. People who didn't practice those poses instead took stances that a lot of people take before an interview. They cross their arms or legs (sort of wrapping themselves up), and maybe look down— at their phones, their notes, or the floor. She sent all the testers into a mock job interview where the interviewer just looked at them without smiling or nodding—just a dead stare.

Power posers felt better after the interview, AND they were more likely to be chosen as the one to hire.

It may feel silly to do, but it's always a good idea to pump up your energy and confidence before an interview. In a video interview, it can really help how you appear on camera.

Whether you power pose or not, I want you to visualize being successful in the interview. Visualization is incredibly powerful. Creating an image of your success in your mind will help create a positive attitude. If you go into an interview with a positive attitude, your breathing will be more natural, you'll smile, your eye contact will be totally appropriate, and you'll appear relaxed, confident, and enthusiastic. All good things.

When to Sign On

About 20 minutes before the interview, sit down, get your computer up and running, and make a quick call to a friend to check that everything's working. Sign into the meeting a minute or two before the interview starts. If you need help to get the timing right, set an alarm 5 minutes before the interview starts.

If you're interviewing with a company in another time zone, double check what time you need to be online the day before. It will be in the email they sent you to invite you to the call.

How to Start an Interview without a Traditional Handshake

In a normal, in-person interview, you would greet your interviewer with the all-important handshake and smile. For a video interview, a cheerful, smiling hello with a look into the camera to make eye contact is great. Say "How are you?" or "It's nice to be here. Thank you for meeting with me."

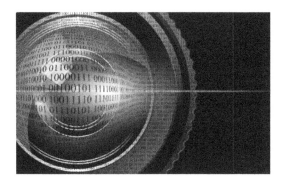

One gentleman I coached had a fabulous resume and fantastic speaking skills, but he wasn't getting hired and could not understand why not. When he hired me to coach him and practice interviewing with him, I could see what the interviewer saw—the tops of his eyelids, for the whole interview. He was looking at his screen so he could see my face, instead of looking into the camera, so I could see his.

This is the #1 issue that I see people not handling well: eye contact. It's so tempting to look at your screen so you can see the interviewer's face and gauge how you're doing. But it hurts you because it makes them feel as if you're not looking them in the eye (because you're not) which can come across as a lack of honesty, as well as a lack of skill with technology.

To have proper eye contact in a video interview, you have to look directly into the lens while you speak. It feels awkward—but it has a big positive impact on how they perceive you. After I pointed this out and practiced with him looking into the lens as he spoke, then he got a great job. Eye contact really matters.

Here's how you do it: Look at the camera lens when you speak, and look at the screen when they're talking to you.

And here's the warning that goes with it: watch out for staring into the camera. Imagine the camera lens is the interviewer's eye. In person, you wouldn't want to intensely stare into their eyes without blinking or breaking contact every little bit. Though the majority of your speaking time should have you looking at the lens, try to find a natural balance between looking into the camera lens and away.

If you have a separate webcam (that isn't built into your computer screen frame), try to keep the camera as close to your screen as possible so you're not moving your head back and forth too far.

If you think you might forget to look into the camera lens while you speak, put sticky notes around it with big arrows pointing to it so you remember to look. If you feel more than a little nervous about talking to the black hole of a camera lens, here's a helpful trick: Put up a picture of someone who encourages you around the camera lens so that you naturally smile and easily look at them when you speak.

Practice Positive Body Language

Interviews are stressful, and interviewing on a screen may feel even less comfortable than in person. Know that you may have to push past that uncomfortable feeling in order to project the confidence you need to in the interview.

Since you're not in the room with them, it's harder for them to pick up on subtle facial expressions. In order to project that image of confident enthusiasm through the screen, don't put on a fake personality, but do focus on being extra alert, happy, confident and relaxed so that you make the best impression.

Before the interview, take a few deep, calming breaths and imagine that the person you're about to speak with is a friend. Remember that they liked your resume and are interested in having this conversation with you. Really focus on expecting a positive outcome from this call.

During the entire interview, sit up straight, with both feet flat on the floor. Choose a chair that encourages that posture, rather than a relaxed slouch. This will keep you properly framed in the screen and make you less likely to fidget. Lean forward toward the camera, just a bit. It will make you seem enthusiastic about the job and approachable.

Find a comfortable position so you don't end up fidgeting or shifting in your seat, because that looks like nerves and uncertainty to them.

I coached one young man who had a pen in his hand that he kept clicking on and off, until suddenly it flew out of his hand. Naturally, he was embarrassed, especially because he hadn't even realized he was holding the pen, much less clicking it.

Nerves are real, and understandable, but do everything you can to minimize any distractions. Resist the temptation to fiddle with papers, touch your face or hair, crack your knuckles, or perform any other nervous tics because those things undermine their perception of you.

A calm, confident demeanor makes you seem trustworthy. Practice keeping your shoulders down and relaxed.

Remember to smile and nod as appropriate. That doesn't mean you have to smile all the way through your interview. However, frequent, naturally-occurring smiling makes you seem friendlier, energetic, approachable, and confident. It helps the person you're smiling at know that you're listening and engaged, and it encourages them to respond positively to you, so you have a better experience. And, it even helps deliver the message to your brain that the situation you're in isn't so bad. Nodding occasionally while they speak to you shows you're actively listening, and can hear them.

Knowing body language tips also help you decipher what they're thinking. Try to pick up cues to see how they're responding to you. Are they leaning forward in interest? Are their eyes looking at something else in their room? You can gauge how you're doing with these kinds of clues.

Check Your Pace

How you sound in your interview is just as important as how you look. Nervous people often rush their speech and you don't want to seem nervous. This is a conversation, after all, just like an in-person interview. Remember to speak in a conversational tone, at a good pace—not too slow or too fast.

If there's any kind of a lag between you, a measured pace will help minimize it. Wait until they're done speaking before you answer. When you finish your answer, smile, nod, or just stop talking.

While you're thinking about your pace, keep an ear out for bad speaking habits.

One of the most notorious bad habits is inserting 'like' excessively into your speech. Many people do it, but it will make you seem nervous or ill-prepared for the interview. Even worse, it stands out more in a video or phone interview than it does in person. So please watch out for that and eliminate it from your speech.

Another especially bad habit that I see all the time is people using speech fillers such as 'um,' 'uh,' in order to fill the silence. This also stands out like a sore thumb in a phone or video interview.

Don't be afraid of the silence. When they ask you a question, it's OK to take a beat or two to compose your answer. When you're done with your sentence, just be quiet. You can smile or nod to indicate that you're done, but don't try to fill the silence. Close your mouth and let that space just sit there. Being OK with the silence communicates confidence.

If it turns out that you need to look something up or check your notes, it's OK to just say so. You'll seem like a great communicator, and they won't worry that the screen froze.

✳✳✳✳✳✳✳✳✳✳✳✳✳✳

If you need a confidence boost for job hunting, interviews, or career advancement, get a copy of my Career Confidence Instruction Manual, available on Amazon and Audible.
- Discover the "rules" restricting your life / career
- Amp up your confidence before any conversation (interviews!)
- Replace the negative voice in your head with a positive one
- Overcome fear or doubt for a more positive outlook
- Get opportunities that have intimidated you up until now
- Inspire others to believe in you and your capabilities

✳✳✳✳✳✳✳✳✳✳✳✳✳✳

66

Ask for the Next Step

When you know you're reaching the end of the call, first you need to verify that you understand what the hiring process is, if you haven't already asked. That means knowing if they have other interviews and when they plan to make a decision and have this position filled. Then, you need to ask for the next step.

Asking for the next step is asking to be moved forward in the process. Most companies won't hire you after this one interview, so likely there would be another conversation required with them or someone else. This would sound something like:

"I'm very excited about the position. I appreciate your time, speaking with you today, and I really want to move forward in the process and get to know more about you, the company, and this opportunity. Based on our conversation, do you feel comfortable moving me to the next step?"

Or:

"Based on our conversation today, do you see me being successful in this role?"

Don't be afraid to ask these questions. You deserve to know the answer. If you haven't made this person want to offer you the job or at least arrange another interview, you need to know why not. It may be something you can correct right then, which will save your spot in this process. If they're on the fence, this may nudge them into going ahead and at least setting up another conversation.

If they won't commit right now and say, "We're not sure yet. We've got to talk to other candidates," that's OK. They may be telling you the truth, or it may be something they automatically say to everyone.

If you're very interested in this job, you can still respond on a positive note by saying something like, "I understand. I do want to say one more time that I am excited about this opportunity. I think it's a perfect fit for me," and then briefly say why.

If you are brand-new to this type of job, you could say, "I have to tell you, Mr. Interviewer, I have never failed in the past and I don't intend to start now. If you hire me, you'll never regret it."

These are the kinds of strong closing statements you need to make. Competition is tough out there. You can't afford not to set yourself apart in this interview process.

When you ask to be moved along, it sets you apart. It shows you as someone who is confident, purposeful, and enthusiastic about the job.

What If It's a Panel Interview?

What happens if your interview is with more than one person? It's not uncommon to have a team on the call from different parts of the company. Typically, it usually consists of three to five people who have different positions within the company that all have a stake in how you will perform your job there. These may include a representative from human resources, the person who will be your supervisor, another member of the team you will be working with, or another person from upper management. For certain fields in academia or science related professions, there could be more of your immediate coworkers and peers in the panel.

It's bad enough to face a panel interview in person, but on a video call, it can be hard to keep track of all the faces on your screen.

Try to find out ahead of time if you're having a panel interview and who will be on the panel. Your contact within the company or your recruiter is the person to ask. If the answer is yes, you need to do a bit more prep work.

Start by looking up each person who will be on the panel on LinkedIn or Facebook to try and get a sense of who they are and what their background is. Know what they do within the organization so that you can speak to each of their interests with your interview answers. Remember that they all want to know how you'll will fit in with their company and culture but also how you'll interact with them personally if they'll be working closely with you. Do as much research as possible, so that you know how it works, what their roles are, and what your role will be in relation to them. The best defense for any situation where you might be nervous is preparation.

How do you keep track of everyone? The good news is that in a multi-screen video call, you're likely to have their names displayed right below their faces on screen, so it's easy for you to remember and address by name the person you're speaking with.

When you're done with the interview, make sure you send each person you interviewed with a thank you note—not just the boss. These should be individualized as much as possible. They will be comparing notes on you, so don't send a form letter.

Panel interviews are notoriously uncomfortable for the interviewee, but the more information you can gather, the better—just like in any interview. Also, just like in any interview, stay calm and steady, breathe, and ask strategic questions. If you think you may be more nervous than in a one-on-one interview, please practice a multi-person call before your interview. That will help.

Mistakes to Avoid—and How to Recover When You Can't

Noisy Disruptions

Even if you've done all you could to send the kids or the dogs away, what happens if they interrupt anyway? Or what if the doorbell rings or someone starts a lawnmower outside your window? It's OK. Stay calm, resolve the situation quickly, apologize for the interruption, and move on. If you have to mute your microphone first, that's OK too.

It's better if those things don't happen in the first place, but the interviewer knows as well as anyone that things don't always happen according to plan. Watching you deal with it quickly and effectively can be a demonstration for them of how you'll handle less-than-desirable pop-up situations on the job.

Technology Fails

If you lose the video and can't get it back quickly, it's OK. Sometimes technology fails. Prepare for disaster. Have the number to call back into that meeting, with the PIN (you'll find it in your Zoom invite). If that doesn't work, have their actual phone number ready so you can just call them quickly and get on with your interview.

If you're there to start the meeting but they aren't, wait a minute or two and then call them to see what's going on. Be proactive and communicate.

If the problem is on your end and you can't fix it fast, it's OK to ask if they would like to reschedule, or do this first interview by phone.

One unfortunate job seeker's technology went bad on her halfway through the interview. She began sounding electronic and stuttering like Max Headroom (ah, the 80s!). She just kept on, and it went so badly that she didn't get another interview. She should have stopped it and asked to reschedule, or switch to a phone call.

Assume that it's your responsibility to make sure this interview goes well. Take control of any unexpected situation. It shows your ability to respond and manage through stressful situations.

You Can't Hear Them

If you find that you can't hear the interviewer, try using the chat feature on Zoom or Skype or whatever it is to let them know you can't hear them. If you've done your practice call ahead of time, you know it's probably not on your end. So maybe the issue is that they hit their mute button and need to unmute. Be patient and don't let this throw you off your game. If you still can't hear, you can suggest that you switch to a phone call. Probably, they will suggest it themselves.

Miscommunication

Communication can suffer when you're not in the same room as the person you're talking to. If you don't understand a question they asked, it's OK to ask them to say it again or clarify. It's appropriate to say, "Do you mean…" or "You're asking…" and then say what it is you think they want to know.

When you finish answering, you can say something like, "Is that the answer you were looking for?" or "Did that address the question properly?" Throughout the interview, you can touch base to see if you're on track by asking questions like, "Is that what you mean?" or "Did I answer that completely?"

Rambling or Blowing an Answer

It's very easy to get nervous in a video interview, because it doesn't feel like a natural way to have a conversation. Remember, don't feel as if you need to fill every moment of silence. It's fine to pause to think, or pause after you answer to let them think or take notes.

If you find yourself rambling off topic, it's OK to just stop. Smile and say, "Did I answer your question?" If you give an answer that you realize isn't what you wanted to say as soon as it leaves your mouth, it's OK to say, "That isn't quite what I wanted to say. What I meant is…" And then go on to give the answer you want to.

How to Follow Up

Following up after your interview is a critical part of the process that employers watch very carefully. They often evaluate how you handle this as a gating factor to eliminate you. If you ignore it, they'll see it as a negative. If you handle it well, it will be another positive check that helps you stand out.

The first step in a good follow up process is sending a thank you note—**within 24 hours of your interview**.

The Thank You Note

Thank you notes are underappreciated by many job seekers. They do so many good things for you—they keep you in the top of the hiring manager's mind, they impress everyone with your good manners, and they give you another opportunity to sell yourself as the best candidate.

As soon as you conclude the call, start writing a substantial thank you note to the person you interviewed with, and email it within 24 hours. If you had a panel interview, email everyone separately.

A word of caution: I once had a candidate who was so concerned about sending it quickly that she wrote it on her phone in a couple of minutes and hit send without checking for typos and spelling errors—and there were a couple. She ended up having to write another note apologizing for the errors that were a result of her extreme enthusiasm. She did end up saving the day and getting the job, but please don't put yourself in that situation. Take the time to edit before you send.

What Should Your Thank You Note Say?

As an overall guide, thank you notes should aim for politeness, directness and clarity.

First, thank them for meeting with you and briefly mention how excited you are about this opportunity.

Then, summarize why you're a great fit as a reinforcement of what you said in the interview. If you thought of something you didn't say but should have, this is your chance to tell them. If you realized you flubbed an answer or made a mistake, this is how you do some damage control.

To close your note, ask for the next step in this process, if you don't already have it set up. If you do, just confirm it.

Sample Thank You Notes

For instance, your note might look something like this:

Ms. Smith,

Thank you for speaking with me today. I'm excited about this job and think I would be a great fit. I really see how my experience in X, Y, and Z can help you meet your goals in A, B, and C. My skills in D, E, and F would be an additional advantage.

I'm looking forward to speaking with you again. I'll contact you in a few days to set it up.

Sincerely,…

Or this:

Mr. Jones,

Thank you so much for speaking with me today. I enjoyed our conversation and I'm even more certain that this is a great fit for us both.

As I'm thinking about it further, it seemed to me that you're most interested in X, with someone who has ABC skills. Because I've developed those skills in previous roles, I know how to get there quickly. I think that working together, we could exceed your expectations.

I would love to speak with you further about how we could achieve your goals. Could we set up a call on Tuesday?

A thank you note like these will showcase your good manners, demonstrate your professionalism, and reinforce the idea that you're a good fit. Even more, they show that you want the job so much that you'll contact them in a few days to keep the conversation going. Enthusiasm can go a long way with hiring managers.

If you didn't get a chance to present your 30-60-90-day plan, you can attach it to your note. You could even update your plan based on your conversation, and attach it with that explanation.

Never fail to send a thank you note after any interview.

After the Note

If you haven't heard back from them by the date they said they would make a decision, it's perfectly acceptable to wait another day and call them directly to ask about it.

Calling to see what's going on isn't pushy—it's good communication, and a proactive move that expresses your continued interest in the position. Don't assume that if they haven't called you to offer you the job that they don't want you. Often, they're just busy. So, make the call and say something like, "I'm very interested in this position and I haven't heard back yet, so I'm wondering where we are with this, or if there are any other questions I can answer for you."

The interview process is a conversation. Do what you can to keep the conversation moving forward, exchanging information until you get to a (hopefully positive) conclusion.

Relax

If you haven't done a video interview before, don't worry—the learning curve seems steeper than it is. Once you get the technical details ironed out and make a few practice calls, you'll feel much better about the entire process.

Before your interview, take time for a few deep, calming breaths. Maybe even stand up and do a Superman power pose for a minute or two. Remind yourself that you can do this. And expect it to go well. You have no reason to think that it won't. They're interested in you, which is why they asked for this call.

Don't forget to use visualization to boost your confidence. Take a minute to think about a time that you felt really powerful or successful and immerse yourself in that memory. Where were you? What were you wearing? Was it sunny, raining, or cold? Really try to put yourself back there. Then think about what you did or what happened that made you feel happy, successful, or powerful. This mental uplift is a great way to start your interview.

****

If you need a confidence boost for job hunting, interviews, and career advancement, please get a copy of my Career Confidence Instruction Manual, available on Amazon and Audible.

I've received some amazing responses from readers about how this helped them. Your mindset, your mental strength, and your confidence affects everything about your job search, your career path, and your life. I urge you to get a copy for yourself.

****

Video Interview Checklist

✓ Download any necessary software
✓ Check your internet connections
✓ Check that your camera, microphone, and speakers are working
✓ Update your computer
✓ Check your background – it should be clean and uncluttered
✓ Secure your camera at a good height
✓ Check your lighting – use a ring light, window light, or multiple lamps for even lighting
✓ Get rid of anyone or anything in the room that could possibly make a noise
✓ Have a great interview!

BONUS – How to Answer 12 Unique Interview Questions About Remote Work

Many jobs interviewing by video are for actual in-office, on-site jobs. But what if you're interviewing for a job where you'll be working remotely on a permanent basis?

Remote work comes with its own unique set of challenges and hiring managers will want to understand how you'll deal with them to be productive and successful in this role.

So, it's important that you're ready to respond to interview questions that deal with the unique issues involved in remote work. In general, you want to approach this set of questions ready to talk about several key points:

- how you're comfortable with technology and with trying new tech;
- how you're aware of the communication roadblocks of remote work versus in-office work and have plans to deal with that; and
- how you can be focused, organized, and productive working from home.

Specifically, here are 15 questions to be ready for:

Why do you want to work remotely?

The truth is that remote work isn't for everyone. It takes a lot of self-motivation and discipline, as well as a certain comfort level with being alone a lot. Especially if you've always worked near others, it can be a difficult adjustment. So naturally, they're going to want to know how and why you're OK with that.

First, start by mentioning how you just really want to work for this company in particular. Then address the remote piece. On a work level, you could talk about how you've found through the pandemic experience or even before that you can be even more productive working from home than in an office situation with the distractions that come with that. This is a clear benefit to the company, and it's always good to point these out in an interview.

On a personal level, you could about how you appreciate the time you gain in your day without a commute—to either get more done or make every minute count. You may have physical limitations that make working from home a necessity. Or it may be that you simply live in a rural area where there aren't that many opportunities available, and so you're very excited about this one.

At this point, don't mention the fact that you need the flexible hours this job provides. Early on, it can sound like you won't be reliable because you have other things in your life that will take priority over work.

If you happen to be interviewing for a role where the remote option is still up in the air because the hiring manager is on the fence about it, you can point out that once they see how much you can accomplish remotely, you're sure they'll feel great about this situation.

Why do you want to work for us?

If they're interviewing for remote jobs, they may very well have some unique qualities that make them appealing for you to work for.

Absolutely do your research on this company so you can point out the qualities that especially appeal to you.

Try to aim for at least 3 reasons you like this company. Maybe you really appreciate the services or products they offer and you'd be excited to represent them. You could be enthusiastic about tackling the specific challenges this company is facing or helping them achieve the goals they've set. Maybe you love the culture and want to be part of it because they have such a great reputation for customer service or employee development or whatever it might be.

This may also be a place where you can talk about being happy that this role is remote because it fits in with your life or where you are geographically, or even talk about the advantages of remote work in terms of more time for you, more productivity for them.

What kind of experience do you have working remotely?

If you have experience working remotely, this is an easy one. Tell them about that work experience while focusing on the positive parts of it, like:

- you've used X, Y and Z tools and technology
- you achieved A, B, and C
- you received great performance reviews, etc.
- you loved it because of how well you were able to work

If you haven't, that's OK. Many people are moving into remote work for the first time and probably will be in the future. You can still give a good answer by talking about any independent projects you've done, freelance work, or things like that.

It would be really helpful if you could talk about how you're ready to go because you're familiar with the technology required for working and communicating remotely and (even more importantly) very comfortable learning new things.

If you can find out what the company uses for project management, messaging, and so on, it would be great to be able to say you're familiar with them. They may have these listed either as required or preferred in their job listing. A few popular tools to be familiar with (besides Skype and Zoom) are:

- Google Suite (Gmail, Drive, Calendar, Hangouts)
- Microsoft Teams
- Dropbox
- Basecamp
- Slack
- Jira
- GoToMeeting
- Loom
- Asana
- Trello

If this all sounds like a foreign language to you, try doing an internet search for "remote work tools" to find lists of popular tools and how they work.

What skills are most important for remote work?

This may be asked more as "What are your strengths for remote work?" but the answer is basically the same either way. Choose the top 3 things that you have that are also especially valuable for this job.

Some skills important for remote work are:

- Communication skills (truly this is one of the most important)
- The ability to work alone, without much direction
- Time management
- Tech skills – being able to learn new apps or software quickly, resolving computer issues, etc.
- Flexibility
- Organization
- Problem solving

- Prioritizing

And I would add to those by talking about how important it is to work on building relationships. It's more difficult to do when you're not in the office with co-workers, having meetings or coffee or even going to lunch. One way to do this is by making an effort at some of the pleasantries that we naturally do when we see other people in person: "Hey, how are you?" "Good morning," "How's your day going?" "How's your family?" Little efforts like these increase the feeling of relationship which directly benefits teamwork.

How will you stay organized/coordinate/communicate remotely?

If this is a new role, or one where you're trying to get them to let you work remotely, they just need to understand how you'll pull this off without something falling through the cracks.

Say that you understand how important it is to stay organized, on track and in touch with the office or team. You have to show your work in a remote setting, so talk about specific ways you can do that. For instance, you can have a digital calendar like a Google Calendar where everyone can see deadlines and meetings. You might have a great project management system where everyone can retrieve/add to projects and leave notes. And always be ready for video calls to answer questions.

A proactive approach to all of these things shows that you're a team player with drive, who understands your part in the success of the organization.

How will you make x happen without being in an office?

How will you get this work done? Alternatively, they may ask about how you'll coordinate with your team or how you'll manage projects and stay on track. Walk them through your process. Really, the steps to getting things done are essentially the same as when you're in the office. You need a plan, coordination, and communication.

Talk about being somewhat of a project manager. Go through the steps of how you'll control the work process and keep everyone informed and moving. How will you communicate with the team? What dashboard will you use to keep everyone informed of what's going on? If you know what method they use, it's great if you can learn about it before the interview.

Talk in detail about the steps you'll follow to keep everyone informed and keep progress moving forward. Break down the (for example) 5 steps you'll follow, and all the sub-steps so you can show exactly what you'll do. Make them as comfortable as possible by letting them in on all the steps of your process.

How will you stay motivated or productive without being in the office?

This can be a tough issue for remote workers and the bosses who get nervous when they can't see you. Your home is full of distractions, from your comfy couch to all the laundry that needs to be done to just the sheer fact that you don't have others near you already working. The hiring manager also wants to know how you'll manage and what you'll need to do it.

One way to address this is by giving examples or telling stories of times you've been self-motivated or taken initiative on projects. You might talk about specific ways you keep yourself on track—maybe a to-do list or the pomodoro method or some other way you've found to stay productive.

It's important to say that you know you need to take steps to regularly stay in touch with your boss and those you work with, and not just hide out. Talk about how you'll regularly check in so they can stay informed about what you're working on, and you can touch base with any team members. Maybe even set alarms for certain times of day to make sure you send messages or other signals that you're actively and visibly working. Checking in through Slack messages, emails, or video, keeps you motivated and accountable while keeping your boss comfortable.

For a smile, you might talk about how your morning protein shake, your lunchtime walk, or your afternoon coffee gives you the energy you need to keep going.

How will you plan and prioritize your work?

This answer should really be no different than the one you'd give if you were working in the office instead of remotely.

With every job, you need to understand what the goals are of your office or management team or company. Their goals are your goals. Make sure you prioritize those over any other sidebar situation that might come up for you in the course of a day, or anything else you might have a chance to participate in. Even a volunteer opportunity that may be great for your career or the community at large can't take priority over what your boss needs to have done.

So, talk about how you'll prioritize based on what your manager or boss wants and make sure to show them what you're doing. If you have a scheduling system that works well for you, you could mention it, or ask what system they use.

What will you do if there's a time-sensitive issue and no one on your team is reachable through normal channels?

One advantage and disadvantage of remote work is that your work hours might not line up with others. This is where being proactive is important. If no one is logged into the project management platform you're using and it's a really critical issue, my recommendation is to go old-school and just call them. Calling is not taboo. I work with people all the time and just pick up the phone and call them. It's not intrusive. They always have the option not to pick up if they can't (for whatever reason). But because I called, they know that I need to speak with them even if they haven't checked their email or whatever and they can call me back when they can.

Do you have a home office set up for this job?

Clearly, if you're working from home, you'll need a space to do it. Some hopping from place to place with your laptop might be OK depending on the role, but if you're working with confidential material or on a lot of calls (video or not), privacy might be an issue.

It's nice if you can talk about your home office as it is already set up, but if not, talk about what you're doing to create a good workspace. It should have doors for privacy so you won't be interrupted, and maybe light or sound items (ring lights, good microphones, rugs or curtains, etc.) that make sure you can have clear, professional work calls. You could talk about your computer and high-speed internet connection, and your organized desk. When you're doing your video interview for the role, you should be in your home office so they can see your setup.

Keep in mind that the issue adjacent to this one is about how you'll keep from being distracted while working from home. So be ready to talk about how you've already thought through how to minimize distractions. For instance, your kids will be at school during the day, your pets have a regular schedule or a dog walker, and if your internet goes out, you have a plan for getting it back fast.

What kind of work schedule do you need?

The ideal answer to questions about your work schedule is, "The schedule you want is the schedule I want."

Some advice you'll find says to talk about the hours you can work right off the bat to make sure you're on the same page, but in my opinion, it's best to delay that discussion until you get them to the point where they want to hire you. It's like talking about salary. They're more likely to be flexible on those things that you want if they've already decided they need you on the team. Bringing it up too soon can give the impression that this role won't be a priority for you.

If you have to ask for a certain schedule, make sure you point out how that will affect them positively—not negatively. "Yes, I need this, but you get X out of it, which would help with Y." Something like that.

What do you see as the biggest potential challenges in remote work and how will you deal with them?

First, don't talk about personal aspects of this, like how it's hard for you to work alone, your dog is rambunctious, or that you need a nap after lunch. Keep this answer focused on the job itself, not on your potential personal weaknesses in doing it.

One of the best ways to focus this answer is to talk about communication. I'm a firm believer that this really is one of the biggest challenges in remote work—all kinds of pieces of that. It's harder to build relationships. There are group think issues and problem-solving issues.

For instance, I've been in offices where when we had a problem, we could put 4-5 people in a room together to brainstorm from a variety of perspectives and rapidly come up with solutions. You can do that online as well, but can feel more difficult if you're not used to that. The way to deal with it is to set plans. If this happens, I'll try X. If that happens, I'll try Y. Think through the possibilities. Have plans to organize the team regularly, and be OK with disbanding quickly if you don't need it or if you get the problem solved fast. This is a very common issue. Many companies are trying to create ways to have group meetings online that feel more personable and comfortable for people to deal with this.

Generally, showing that you're aware of these kinds of issues like communication, proactively thinking about solutions, and ready to implement whatever works to solve them is a good answer.

BONUS – Job Interview Prep Kit

How to Do Your Company Research

*Complete a Company Overview
-Find the Company on LinkedIn – read posts
-Parent Company?
-Subsidiary of? (+ trading symbol, if public)

*Key Numbers to Know:
-Company Type (Public, Private, Venture Capital)
-Employee Count
-Current/Most Recent Sales
-Current/Most Recent Net Income
-1 Year Sales Growth
-1 Year Net Income Growth
-1 Year Employee Growth
-Fiscal Year End

*Identify the Decision Makers
-Who is/are the hiring manager(s)?
-What is their title and past experience?
-How long have they been there?
-Where is their location?
-Who do they report to?
-Who is the Human Resources contact?

*Identify Competitors
-Who are the company's top 3 competitors?
*Identify Product Line / Services
-What are the company's top products or services?
-Are there any new products in development?

*Do a SWOT Analysis of the Product/Service/Company/Opportunity
        -**Strengths**
        -**Weaknesses**
        -**Opportunities**
        -**Threats** (Don't forget reimbursement challenges, newer technology, market conditions, etc.)

*Determine why you're a fit for this position
        Be specific. Know your skill set and how it compares to the skill set required for the position. (See the job description for clues.)

Questions to Ask During the Interview

- Why is the position open?
- Where will the job be performed? Is it based at headquarters or is it field-based?
- What do they see as the primary focus for this position? What is the greatest challenge?
- When do they want to have someone in the position?
- How long have they been looking?
- Can you describe the best performer that you have on your team in a similar role?
- What will the interview process be?
- What are the goals they want to accomplish?
- How do they see the position developing? (Growth Path)

How to Use LinkedIn for Company Research

LinkedIn is a great place to do research on a prospective company. For example, say you were interested in Stryker. You'd search the name of the company.

Notice that your search brings up other divisions of the company that you may not have been aware of before. When you click on the company name, it will take you to the company's corporate webpage, where you'll find all kinds of information about the company, including links to current employees.

Scroll down further, and you'll see updates on company activities. You might see information on new hires, promotions, changes, projects, company events, or even financial news.

Check out the employees' links, and you'll see employee profiles that could tell you what kind of person they like to hire. What is the median age? Do you see a gender slant? Do they have similarities in background? These are indicators of culture.

If it's a large company, you might consider reaching out to those who are or were in a similar position as the one you're considering. But be careful! Don't reach out to the person IN the position you're applying for. If he or she has been let go, you may not get an objective opinion.

Try someone in the same position (but another location) and explain that you're considering a position with the company and want to get their advice on the company, position, etc. How do you contact these folks? If you're connected, it's easy to message them. If you're not connected, you can ask to connect. If you're not connected but are in the same LinkedIn group, you can message them there.

What should you ask one of these contacts? Questions you might ask a current or past employee of your prospective employer:

    1. How long have you been there?
    2. How did you get hired?
    3. What do/did you love about the company?
    4. What do/did you not love?

5. What can you tell me about the job?
6. Do you know the manager (in your area)?
7. Is there any advice you could give me?
8. What about the "x" product or service?
9. How is the environment/culture?
10. Who are the competitors?

How Does Your Experience Fit This Position?

Match the key requirements to your experience:
*Job Title
*Job Description (Summary) = Your Experience
*Primary Responsibilities = Your Current/Similar Responsibilities
*Key Requirements = Your Background (Education/Certification and Minimum Experience)

Interview Questions You May Be Asked:

1. Why do you want to work here? This is where your research will reward you – give specific examples of what appeals to you about this company and this job.

2. Why did you leave your last job? / Why are you looking to leave? Don't say anything negative about your previous employer, but be honest – is it salary, career growth, travel requirements, etc.?

3. What can you do for us that other candidates can't? Be specific – give an example of a success you had in the past that helped or improved a process, boosted revenue, etc.

4. What salary are you seeking? It's best to deflect, but if they ask for a specific number, it's fine to answer: "I'm currently making ___," or "In my last position my salary was ___, and I am open to a reasonable offer within that range."

5. What would your prior manager say about you? Point out your strengths and any success you had.

6. Describe a work-related issue or problem you had to face recently. How did you deal with it? This is seeking to evaluate your decision-making ability. Give an example where you had a positive impact on a situation. Use the STAR method to structure your answer.

7. What type of Supervisors or Managers have you found it easiest or most difficult to work with? This is searching for your adaptability. Be specific on what works for you. Example: Gives clear direction, is specific on expectations, etc.

8. What was the best decision you ever made? What were the alternatives? How did you go about making it? This is checking for your judgment.

Developing Your Success Story

In the interview, choose stories to tell that illustrate your proficiencies in the topics important in the position for which you are interviewing. Some possible areas are listed below, but feel free to include your own to highlight your strengths (not all topics will apply).

Strengths as an Employee:
  - What have others said about you?

- Reviews – Do you have reviews or evaluations you can refer to?
- Recommendations
- What do you do?

Management Style:
- How did you handle conflicts among coworkers?
- What goals did you put in place for your team?
- How did you delegate assignments or territories?
- How do you evaluate employees?
- What did you look for in someone to hire?

Marketing Experience:
- How did you determine where to go?
- What tools did you develop?
- What strategies did you use?

Leadership:
- Did you motivate others?
- Did you mentor or train others?

Creativity:
- What tools did you develop?
- How did you strategize?
- What makes you different?

Technical Expertise:
- What specific or specialized training do you have?

Dependability:
- Give examples of what you did.

Other Topics to Consider:
- Are you a team player?
- How did you learn from mistakes?
- Character?
- Mergers/ acquisitions?
- Crisis management?
- New product development?
- New product introduction?
- Product life cycle?
- QSR?
- Quality?

10 Common Interview Questions

PRACTICE, PRACTICE, PRACTICE your answers to interview questions!

- *Tell me about yourself.* Point out areas of success (career growth path, strategy, follow-through, work ethic).

- *Why have you had so many / so few jobs?* Give an example of how you manage your time well (give example of multi-tasking).

- *What's the biggest mistake you've ever made?* Nothing damaging…but what you learned.

- *What is your greatest accomplishment?* Choose examples that demonstrate key "hiring characteristics."

- *What are your strengths?* Choose strengths that would help you succeed in this job.

- *What do you need to work on?* Use a strength that you could improve.

- *How do your co-workers describe you?* Team player, outgoing, dedicated, etc.

- *What new goals have you set for yourself lately?* Be specific.

- *Why should we hire you?* Give examples of how you are equal to their requirements, plus a little bit more, if you can.

Be descriptive. Don't just answer "yes" or "no" to questions. But also avoid over-answering. Make your answers colorful but not lengthy.

Sell yourself to the interviewer, but without exaggeration or telling lies. You are there to market yourself, blow your own horn and explain why you'd be right for the role. But don't come across as arrogant.

Avoid making negative remarks about your current employer, past employers, or colleagues. This will only reflect badly on you in the interview.

Be determined. Make it clear that you want to get the job, even if you are given information in the interview that sheds a new (negative) light on the role. Be positive, and then evaluate the opportunity again when you are away from the interview. Don't burn your bridges.

Have positive body language, and maintain a good posture.

More Interview Appearance and Presence Tips...

- Hands should be well-manicured. For nail polishes, choose subtle low-key colors over bright fashion colors.
- Have neat, clean hair with a recent cut and styling.
- Makeup should be light and natural-looking. Avoid excessive makeup.
- Use deodorant and avoid cologne or fragrances.
- Blue, grey or black suits are always in style and the safest, most conservative choice. Be sure it's cleaned and pressed. Shirts should be white or light blue, freshly laundered and well-pressed. Skirts should be around knee-length.
- A quiet tie with a subtle design and a hint of red is suitable for a first interview. Avoid loud colors and busy designs.
- A closed-toe shoe that is color-coordinated with your outfit is appropriate for an interview. Avoid open-toed shoes or sling-backs.
- Shoes should be freshly polished (including the heels). Socks should match or coordinate with your suit and worn over the calf.
- Jewelry should be kept minimal. A watch and wedding or class ring are acceptable. Don't wear jewelry or pins that indicate membership in religious or service organizations.
- Practice good posture and be aware of non-verbal communication.
- Maintain good eye contact.
- Turn off all cell phones.

What to Take with You
- Resume(s)
- Brag Book(s) (or other evidence)
- References
- 30/60/90-day plan(s) and/or any other documents/ tools that help you demonstrate your talents and skills
- A brown or black leather portfolio to keep your papers in

Just a Reminder
- Leave early for the interview so you don't arrive late.
- Schedule nothing around your interview that will create a time crunch.
- Don't park at a short-term meter or in a tow zone.
- Use the restroom before you go into the interview.
- No gum, cigarettes or tobacco.
- No sunglasses.
- Turn off your cell phone.
- Wear conservative business attire.
- Get a haircut if you need one.
- No fragrances.
- Never ask to use their phone.
- Don't look at your watch.
- Maintain eye contact, but don't stare.
- Listen intently, so you don't have to keep repeating, "I'm sorry, but could you say that again?"
- Ask for the spelling of the interviewer's name and write it down. (or get their business card)
- Don't ask about money.
- Don't mention a salary range in your resume or during an interview.

- Don't talk about personal problems.
- Don't take anyone else with you to the interview.
- Don't drop names.
- Keep your eyes off the interviewer's desk.
- Don't handle anything, especially personal belongings.
- Never be sarcastic.
- Never criticize anyone, especially an employer.
- If asked to complete a form or application, fill in every space. Never write: "See resume."

Additional Resources

****

Career Confidential Home Page

Find job search tips, strategies, and tools, as well as opportunities for group or private coaching, and free training webinars.

CareerConfidential.com

****

Read more about 30-60-90-day plans here:

https://careerconfidential.com/30-60-90-day-plans-for-job-interviews-top-10-posts/

Or get my proven 30-60-90-Day Plan Template with detailed strategies and tips for using it in any job interview. Each plan comes with a personal review of your completed plan (optional) and a 100% money-back guarantee.

Action Plan (for any white-collar job) -
https://careerconfidential.com/306090-action-plan-product-reviews/
Sales Plan (for sales roles) -
https://careerconfidential.com/306090-sales-plan-product-reviews/
Manager Plan (for management-level and above) -
https://careerconfidential.com/30-60-90-day-plan-for-managers-product-reviews/
Executive Plan (for Directors, VPs, CEOs, etc.) -
https://careerconfidential.com/30-60-90-day-plan-for-executives-product-reviews/

****

Job Search, Career, and Interview Coaching with Peggy McKee

Contact me at coachpeggymckee@gmail.com or find me on LinkedIn: https://www.linkedin.com/in/peggymckee1

Send me a message! I'd love to help you! If you have an interview coming up fast, please let me know and I'll fit you in as fast as I can.

I work with jobseekers all the time on this very thing and it's amazing how much improvement you can get by working with a coach.

How can a coach help you?

- Interviewing skills—both video and on-site
- Better explanation for a layoff or termination
- Get past age discrimination
- Transition to a new career field
- Strengthen your resume & LinkedIn profile to get more interviews
- Build your confidence
- Negotiate salary

One of my favorite stories involves a man who was interviewing for a job with his dream company. He absolutely wanted this job, but he really needed more money. And he was wary of negotiating because he did not want to lose this offer. I spent one hour with him working on good negotiation skills and he ended up with a compensation package more than $50,000 higher than their initial offer.

If you're not convinced yet, find out more about what coaching can do for you here: https://careerconfidential.com/peggy-mckee-career-coaching-special-offer/

Check out my group coaching memberships! https://careerconfidential.com/coaching-memberships-nf/

****

Other Peggy McKee Books available on Amazon

Career Confidence Instruction Manual

5-Star Reviews on Amazon!

"If you are struggling with getting things done, and realize you lack confidence and the strength…if you have plenty of confidence and want to maintain and expand it, this book is for you…talking about confidence so clearly, practically, and usefully…Everyone knows they cannot succeed with negative attitudes and without trying - hard. But lots of folks develop poor thought patterns anyway, and underachieve, and that's a shame. This book, with…exercises and specific action plans, can help you overachieve…get the most from your efforts."

How to Answer Interview Questions

"I highly recommend this book. It has a multitude of helpful suggestions…I felt truly prepared for any type of interview question. I understood what information the interviewer was trying to gather from the question and how to respond to present myself in the best possible manner. I landed a job using this book and I will refer back to it throughout my career. Great resource!"

How to Answer Interview Questions II

"I wish I would have read this book before going on my past job interviews! I just laughed when I recognized the many mistakes that I made in answering difficult questions. This book gave so much knowledge and insight into appropriate answers that interviewers look for from potential job candidates. I would recommend this book to all job seekers!"

About the Author

Peggy McKee has been guiding job seekers through a fast, successful job search process since 1999 as a recruiter and career coach. She's been recognized by CNN as a national job search authority, and was named by HR Examiner as the #1 Most Influential Online Recruiter. Her eBooks are available on Amazon and Audible. As the CEO of Career Confidential, she's helped over 29,000 customers in over 92 countries around the world, and hundreds of thousands of readers and viewers on our blog and YouTube channel.

If You Liked This eBook, Please Give It 5 Stars!

Reader reviews are so important...both for the success of this book and for me, so I know that I've given you what you need to be successful in online interviews. If you put the tips and principles of this book into practice and it results in an amazing interview for you, let me know!

Please review this book on Amazon!

Also, look for my additional Amazon books on a variety of other job search and career topics.

14013405R00059